SECRE

Secrets

R.H. Dewhirst

love always

Vic x.

PUBLISHED BY THE AUTHOR'S FAMILY

This compilation of poems by R. H. Dewhirst
first published 2011

Published by the author's family
Oakfell, Littlefell Lane
Lancaster, LA2 0RG

ISBN: 978 0 9568929 0 4

Book design and production for the publishers by
Bookprint Creative Services <www.bookprint.co.uk>
Printed in Great Britain.

ROBERT HEDLEY DEWHIRST

Robert Hedley Dewhirst was born in Embsay, near Skipton, North Yorkshire on 24 September 1918. He left school at the age of thirteen and went to work as a warehouse boy in one of the many cotton mills in Skipton.

In 1937 he joined the Royal Army Medical Corps. In World War II he saw service in the Middle East and Germany. After the war he moved with his wife, Winnie, to Lancaster, where he trained as a plumber. He lived the rest of his life in Lancaster but never forgot his roots in Yorkshire.

His poetry reflects his life, his thoughts and his love of the countryside. He died in Lancaster on 13 February 2008.

CONTENTS

Mugwumps' Picnic

Kate arranged with the Mugwumps
A picnic one day
Over the hills
And far away

And soon all assembled
And ready for off
Kate smartly dressed up
She looked quite a toff

The Mugwumps all tidy
In their Sunday suits
Hair neatly combed
And lovely clean boots

The Mugwumps expectant
And somewhat presumptuous
They all looked ahead
To something quite scrumptious

So off to the country
They went with a scamper
The Mugwumps all helping
To carry the hamper

They found a green field
Where they could all dine
With a tablecloth cover
Of sweet celendine

The Mugwumps knew Kate
She'd not let them down
Starters of sandwiches
White bread or brown

There were sugary buns
With cherries on top
Lashings of trifle
And bottles of pop

All kinds of biscuits
And gingerbread men
Some small Easter eggs
And a large chocolate hen

Lots of fresh cream
With jelly and custard
And, for some unknown reason
A small pot of mustard

Some apples and oranges
Bananas and pears
And creamy inviting
Chocolate eclairs

Soon the feast was all over
Nothing left but the crumbs
And some rather strange rumbles
From some rather fat tums

What are your names
Kate guilelessly said
They shouted in chorus
We all answer to Fred!

These similar names
Were extremely confusing
So they played many games
Which was much more amusing

Their games were quite robust
Like tiggy and rounders
And leapfrog, of course
For these little bounders

Then Mugwumps, mischievous
As Mugwumps can be,
All climbed to the top of
A very tall tree

They climbed so high
That they couldn't see town
And, yes! You have guessed it
They couldn't get down!

So Kate once more
To the rescue did run
She thought it was serious
They thought it was fun!

Alas! Like good things
It all had to end.
In the cool of the evening
They homeward did wend

Kate said 'Goodbye'
Her eyes dewy with tears
The Mugwumps all gave her
A rousing 'three cheers'

They gave their farewells
With kisses unending
Which helps me to rhyme
A nice happy ending

The Mugwumps
For Kate – February 1981

The Mugwumps went sailing
One day for a lark
Upon a large lake
They had found in the park

They had an old box
Which they used for a boat
They hadn't a sail
So they used an old coat

For such a long journey
They took something to eat
A few loaves of bread
And some slices of meat

After sailing some time
With the sun shining bright
Feeling quite hungry
They stopped for a bite

Soon . . . all one could hear
Was 'gobble' and 'munch'
When suddenly came
A most horrible crunch!

They'd been so busy eating
It seemed no one was thinking
To keep a look out. . .
And now they were sinking!

For their boat had contacted
(I'm sorry to say)
A rather large rock
That stood in its way

And soon they were calling
'Help! Help us, please!'
As the water rose slowly
Right up to their knees . . .

For Mugwumps, we all know,
Are really quite dim
And none of them ever
Had learned how to swim

Now little Kate Carney
Was just passing by
To the Mugwumps' relief
She heard their faint cry

Kate sped at full speed
To the scene of disaster
She went like the wind
She'd never run faster

Quickly Kate slipped off
Her stockings and shoes
She must save the Mugwumps
She had no time to lose

Kate waded out
And soon she was out, in
The place where the Mugwumps
Were kickin' and shoutin'

She picked up the Mugwumps
There seemed Mugwumps galore
And carried them safely
Back to the shore

The Mugwumps were soaking
And started to cough
So Kate used her hankie
And dried them all off

And then, with a smile
She said, 'Please follow me
We'll go to the caff
For a nice cup of tea'

Now the Mugwumps were happy
And how they loved Kate
They danced round her feet
Singing, 'Isn't she great!'

With a slop and a slurp
They each, gave Katie a kiss
To show they were grateful
To this brave little Miss

But soon it was time
For the Mugwumps to go
To wherever they live
Which, alas, I don't know

Yet, before they departed
Kate said, looking quite grim,
'You must not sail again
Till you've learned how to swim'

The Mugwumps all promised
Then waved Kate goodbye
And Kate watched them leave
With a tear in her eye

Now I have heard rumours
Which in legend are set
That, though Mugwumps aren't thinkers
They never forget

And round Mugwump firesides
They oft still relate
How once they were rescued
By brave little Kate

Northland

Rural scene, Pennines green
Limestone walls and waterfalls

Farmhouse fields, autumn yields
Bracken, wild rose, flowery hedgerows

Viking villages, monuments, images
Rabbits and burrows, tractor-made furrows

Stony fells, churches, bells
Cathedral spires, telephone wires

Stately homes, castles, domes
Harbours, ports, roman forts

Viaducts, bridges, windswept ridges
Potholers, hikers, motorists, bikers

Barking dogs, shawls and clogs
Witches and brooms, shuttles and looms

Satanic mills, chesty ills
Places of history, places of mystery

Hills and dales, sunshine, gales
Heather and clover, curlew, plover

Birthplace of rivers that die by the sea
The north is the Pennines; the Pennines are me

Where Does a Girl . . . ?

Where does a girl who can't pay her rent wear her
    jewellery?

In arrears [in her ears]

From This Window . . .

From this window, I spy
A busy store, and cars pass by
A spreading tree, on whose branches – I can
    see . . .
A group of starlings, slyly looking back at me
Cyclists riding to and fro'
Bounding dogs, when leads let go
Riders on their horses bobbing
Up and down on patient Dobbin
Eager joggers running by
At my ease, I wonder why
Unwary insect to deceive
A spider spins a deadly weave
Thoughts deceitful, dark and deep
Making promises we cannot keep
Truth does not always win the race
When evil sports an honest face

Land of Oz

A funny place, Australia
In the Antipodes
With lots of booze and kangaroos
And eucalyptus trees
And people who go walkabout
Called Aborigines

Girls

Mary? I forget her name
With that lovely golden mane
Of hair . . .
Like falling rain
Caught in the sun
Or, sometimes, fastened in a bun
That lovely face . . . In
A lovely frame
Mary . . . Mary, what's-her-name?

Frogspawn

One day I saw a little frog
Sat upon . . . a lily pad
I thought, were I a tadpole
It might have been my dad!

Perhaps it was a lady frog
I can't tell one from t'other
Then, of course, I do suppose
It might have been my mother!

The Famous

The famous – all in state do lie
Are they favoured, in the sky?
More humble folk like you and I
Look sadly on, and wonder why

But when all is done and all is said
Rich or poor, they're just as dead

Grandmother

Though spring is past
And winter's here a while
Autumn lingers in her eyes
And summer's in her smile

After the Rain

After sudden rain a clear autumn night
The jewels of heaven are shining bright
The milky way a sparkling ring
Scattered pearls from broken string
Magic lanterns held by unseen hands
Countless as the grains of desert sands
The moon reflecting gold in limpid pools
Grows fainter with the passing hours
Yet fainter, still . . . as dewdrops
Settle on the flowers

Cat and Mouse
'Now let's not be hasty. . . . Let's
stop for a chat'

There were creaks and groans
From the old building, it seems,
As it painfully stretched
Its rheumaticky beams

Disturbing the quiet
Of a still, moonless night
To some it could cause
A bit of a fright

But it had no effect
On a very small mouse
Who, looking for goodies
Had entered the house

Now the house was well guarded
From intruders like that
By a quite, rather large
And vicious, tom cat

Who at that moment,
Sad to relate,
For such an event
Was lying in wait

The mouse, unaware
Of the danger he faced
With unerring instinct
To the larder he raced

'Ha-ha,' said the pussy cat
'What have we here?
An unwanted intruder
This do I fear'

The pussy cat smiled
With a sharp-toothed grin
Which seemed to say, oddly
'Be pleased to come in'

Now the mouse being hungry
And most fond of cheese
Said, very politely
'May I pass, if you please?'

'Your wish isn't granted
Your request I decline
I'm the only one here
Who is likely to dine'

Now the mouse had no doubt
After such a broad hint
That he'd be the meat course
That went with the mint

'Say goodbye,' said the cat
'And farewell to strife
For this is the end
Of your miserable life'

'Wait. Wait!' cried the mouse
'Let's stop for a chat;
Politics, religion,
Something like that'

The night had been lonely
For poor pussy, you see.
So, before taking action
He said, 'I agree'

'The folk who live here
Their blood is quite blue.
They will not take kindly
To vermin like you'

The mouse said, astounded,
'You're a Siamese cat
The last who should utter
A remark such as that!'

And continued, 'I am English,'
And, bulging with pride
'Give way to your betters
And please step aside'

'I suggest,' said the mouse
'We both play a game,
It's really good fun
Hide and seek is its name'

'I know it,' the cat said
'I'll count to ten
And as soon as I find you,
For you it's "Amen"'

The cat opened his eyes
And quickly looked round
But the wee little mouse
Was not to be found

Much worse still
And bound not to please
The larder was missing
A large wedge of cheese!

On happy ending
Which good tails are built on
Was a fat little mouse
With a tum full of stilton!

Legendary Witch
for Victoria

I'm told there's a witch
Who lives in a wood;
Whatever she's up to
I'm sure it's no good.
She stirs a big stew pot
With her magic brew,
And if you're not careful
She'll be stirring you!

Her brew is a potion
That's not very nice
Frogs' legs and toadstools
Birds' wings and mice
If you'd like to try it
Beware if she asks
Just politely explain
That you're on a diet

She may appear generous
And ask you to lunch
But it's her jaws you'll hear
When it comes to the crunch.
So to have a good meal
Best pick a good venue
If you lunch with the witch
You'll end up on the menu

The witch is quite ugly
Has a long, hooky nose.
She wears a black cloak
Right down to her toes.
She has a big mouth
And a horrible grin
Don't go too near . . . or
It might gobble you in

Oh, those shoe-button eyes
With her muddy complexion
One sight is enough
If it's in your direction.
Just jump on your bike
And pedal like mad;
Head quickly for home
And dear Mam and Dad

This witch lives alone
In a tumbledown shack
And smoke from her chimney
Is evil and black.
Please don't grow curious
Or look in her door
Or, alas, you might find
You won't grow any more

When the moon's shining bright
You may see her fly,
Perched on her broomstick,
Across the night sky.
With her black cat behind

And her cloak blowing free,
I don't know about you
But she terrifies me

I'm told there's a witch
Who lives in a wood.
I hope you don't meet her,
But if ever you should
Be brave, but be careful
And remember my warning,
Keep clear of her mouth
If you see her yawning

Dawn

See the treetops shyly peering
Above the mist that's slowly clearing
Golden rays now appearing
Heralding another dawn

Morning dew the world is steeping
Leaves and grass genly weeping
Everything is so in keeping
With another lovely morn

Hear the rooster boldly calling
He knows well the stars are falling
Giving us his joyful warning
That another day is born

5th of November

Bonfires and fireworks
The fifth of November
Hot roast potatoes
Guy Fawkes to remember

He came from Yorkshire
With solemn intent
To destroy with gunpowder
The King's Parliament

As history has told us
He didn't succeed
But why we all celebrate
Is a mystery indeed

In view of the antics
Of each politician
To make all this fuss
Is a curious decision

Hear my lament . . . as
To despair I am driven:
Come back dear Guy Fawkes
All is forgiven

Nursery Rhyme

A pussy cat sat on the mat
It said, 'Me-ow, purr, purr'
And things like that

A little dog barked, 'Yap, yap, yap'
A woodpecker went, 'Tap, tap, tap'
A mournful cow called, 'Moo, moo, moo'
A lonely owl sang, 'Twit ta-woo'
A little lamb cried, 'Baa, baa, baa'
A laughing man went, 'Ha, ha, ha'
The little children out at play
They made noises all the day

But pussy cat, sat on the mat
And said, 'Me-ow, purr, purr'
And things like that

I Knew a Man

I knew a man who was rather thin
And a man who was rather tall
I knew a man who was rather fat
And a man who was rather small
Each had a name that didn't match
The way they looked at all
The thin man's name, I think, was Stout
And the tall man's name was Small
The fat man's name, I'm sure, was Slim
The small man's name I can't recall
There's also a man who hadn't been born
So he had no name at all!

There Was a Young Man from Lahore

There was a young man from Lahore
Who worked in a gunpowder store
A quite careless bloke
He stopped for a smoke
You won't see *him* any more

Ambition

When I grow up there's lots of things
That I would like to do
And if you have the patience
I'll tell them all to you

I think I'd like to be a poet
Write an epic . . . something grand
But I shall only use small words
That all can understand

Perhaps I'll be a painter
With paints: blue, red, and green
And paint the finest picture
That you have ever seen

Maybe I'll be a sculptor
And work hard every day
Make grand and noble statues
From out of common clay

Perhaps I'll turn to music
To tantalise your ear
With the music of the masters
The tunes that you hold dear

I'd like to be an architect
Construct a building high
I'm not sure how I'd do it
But I'd like to have a try

I would tell you lots of things
But no more can be said
My mummy's here and she insists
That I must go to bed

Limerick

There was a young fellow named Fred
'I've a terrible headache,' he said
He pleaded again and again,
'Would we please stop the pain.'
So, kindly, we cut off his head

Appearance

They say it's the clothes
That make the man
Fine features the mask of a lover
But like a book . . .
. . . by far
The contents are
More important than the cover

Ego – à la Lewis Carroll

Reflected in the mirror
He saw a strange old man
Quaintly dressed with woolly hat
He looked just like an elf
He looked again and realised
He was looking at himself
The shock was so unnerving
He took a swig of rum
And pleased to say
This soon restored
His e-qui-li-bri-um

Were We?

Were we what we wish to be
Would we be happy then?
To dream a while
May oft beguile
Perhaps we'd wish again

Ad Infinitum

. . . to sow the seed, to reap the wheat
To bake the bread, that we may eat.
The food we eat, this makes us strong,
Thus we can toil our whole life long . . .
To sow the seed . . .

Walking in Silverdale – Spring

Hear the cuckoo calling
It's message sweet and clear
Ambassador with joyful news
To tell us, 'Spring is here'

Feel the west winds blowing
As scattered raindrops squall
Quenching nature's mighty thirsty
Wherever they might fall

See how the buds are springing
The trees will soon be dressed
Some mystic hand, the bluebells ring
To wake them from their rest

See the joyous lambs at play
The hedgerows start to bloom
This most magical of seasons
Breaks out from winter's gloom

We feel our steps grow lighter
The air so bright and clear
As we absorb our blessings
In the springtime of the year

Walking in Silverdale – Summer

Above us in its splendour
The sky in radiant hue
The sun a golden ship becalmed
Upon a sea of blue

A friendly form upon our way
Where we can take our rests
Enjoy nature's gifts around us
Whilst we are nature's guests

In solitude – but happy
We sit there, Win and me
And quietly watch a wildflower
Dispensing pollen to a bee

See the cattle grazing
The grass so fresh and green
We see the heat haze rising
On the road where we have been

Far across the meadow
We hear a faint bell's sound
And in the leafy branches
Songbirds are all around

Hear the toneless droning
The sound that summers bring
We quickly turn; but fail to see
The insect on the wing

Golden moments treasured
As we wander on our way
The greatest gift of nature:
An English summer's day

Walking in Silverdale – Autumn

Walking in Silverdale
Summertime is fading
Winter's drawing nigh
Migrant birds are calling
Wheeling through the sky

Trees, their naked branches,
Reaching up so high
As if to catch the white clouds
Gently sailing by

Autumn leaves go rustling
Blowing round our knees
Gently twisting, turning
Playthings of the breeze

How beautiful the picture
How our eyes are blessed
See nature's transformation
As she . . . prepares to rest

Summertime is fading
Winter's almost here
But memories of autumn
Are the ones we hold most dear

Walking in Silverdale – Winter

Winter time's upon us
A time of rain and snow
The crisp, fresh air is painting,
On our cheeks, a rosy glow

Feel the cold wind blowing
Lowering clouds pass by
Hear winter's cold and icy breath
Through leafless treetops sigh

See the snowflakes falling
From out of a leaden sky
Like seeds they're being planted
From some gardener there, on high

How quickly they are rooted
How quickly they all grow
Soon all the world about us
Is overgrown with snow

See the tiny footprints
Across the snow so bare
Some little woodland creature
Has ventured from its lair

Hear the robin singing
Its redbreast cheers our eyes
Just one of winter's blessings
That no one can disguise

Winter can be so beautiful
But can be so unkind
And lingering thoughts of summer
Keep passing through the mind

1978

Grandparents are we
Grandchildren our joy
Four little girls and one little boy

First there's Victoria
With cute, freckled nose
Fresh as the springtime
Our own English rose

The second, Louise,
Blonde and petite
Smiling blue eyes
And ever so sweet

Third, then, is Kate
Hair all a curl
Among the best gems
There's always a pearl

Fourth we have Robert
A straw-headed boy
As bright as a button
A bundle of joy

Fifth little Emma
So cuddly is she
A beautiful blossom
On our family tree

You

Beside the lake
Tranquil, blue
Smooth, glossy sheet
In which reflected – you
I see, upturned, a perfect image,
Beautiful and still . . . until
Tormented by a passing breeze
Undulating ripples play
Impatiently I wait
Vision lost awhile . . . and then
The wavelets stay, and they
Reflect once more
The perfect form – of you
That I adore

Shipwreck

See the once-proud sailing ship
Struggling with the storm
The rigging's strewn about the deck
Soon she'll be a total wreck
There'll be many we must mourn

The waves like cruel talons
Clutching at her sides
See the lonely mariner – he is lashed
To what remains . . . of a once-tall mast
As he prays the storm she'll ride

See the terrifying wave
That's raised before her prow
Tons of water down will thunder
None can help, she must go under
What can save her now?

How terrible . . . and majestic
This scene we'll always treasure
The artist with his skill has caught
Upon the painting we have bought
She'll ride the waves for ever

Canterbury Avenue

Have you ever seen our houses
They are pretty, trim and neat
Lined up so very smartly
On each side of the street

It's really called an avenue
A name that's meant to please
But whoever named it 'avenue'
Forgot to plant the trees

The roofs secure with slate or tile
In colours red or grey
All topped off with chimney pots
To take the smoke away

Large square-eyes the windows
With which to see the view
With curtains just like eyelids
And walls so strong and true

Some have pleasant little lawns
Like aprons round their waists
Some have rockery and flowers
According to their tastes

It has its share of cats and dogs
And little children too
And, of course, the hoi polloi:
The likes of me and you

Have you ever seen our houses
Standing calm and still
A castle and a refuge
For all of us until . . .

Fidelity

'Oh, little frog, why do you weep
Why shed your froggie tears?'
He looked at me with sad, round eyes
And croaked into my ears

'So long ago, when we first met
In this quiet and peaceful pool
With my lady-love I languished
In its waters deep and cool

'So many little tadpoles
Between us we have spawned
Since that happy springtime
When light of love first dawned

'Alas, my lady-love is gone
To the great pool in the sky
Or wherever little froggies go
When little froggies die'

I have heard these tiny creatures
Are faithful unto death
And knew that he would sorrow
Until his final breath

I thought of words of comfort
Then saw . . . there's nought to say
In pining for his lost love
Little frog had passed away

I felt so sad and helpless
I could only stand and stare
And ponder on the tragic end
He'd reached in his despair

Yet – oh, how misplaced sorrows
Our emotions can beguile
On his lifeless little face . . . I saw
A contented, froggie, smile

Heavenly Flowers

Midst grasses so green
There to behold
Daisies so white
And buttercups gold
Reflected from heaven
Refreshed by the dew
Cornflowers, violets
Forget-me-nots too
Touched by the sunlight
The yellowish glow
Where cowslips mellow
And primroses grow
Pimpernels scarlet
As red sky at night
The hips and the haws
And poppies so bright
A rainbow of colour
Our joy to enhance
Flowers so graceful
In warm breezes dance

Hedgerows of Autumn

The threshold of autumn
We cross with a smile
The hedgerows of England
Accompany each mile

The verdant, tall grasses
Their blades reaching high
Like the arms of the faithful
Towards the blue sky

On the branch of the brier
The wild rose a spray
Of pink and white blossoms
That garnish our way

The fruits of the hawthorns
Re-ripened and red
Wild flowers a-blooming
Adorn their green bed

The threshold of autumn
We cross with a smile
The hedgerows of autumn
Enchant and beguile

Indifference

The auction room was busy
I bid for what I sought
A faded, old, framed photograph
The only thing I bought

The photograph was faded, brown
The time . . . perhaps Victorian
Of this, of course, I can't be sure
As I am no historian

It showed a fine and handsome man
His suit . . . a bygone style
Behind his bland expression – showed
A slight self-conscious smile

His hair was centre-parted
Moustaches neat and trim
His clothing quite immaculate
He was tall and rather slim

A somewhat ornate table – for
One hand to rest upon
The other in his jacket front
à la the great Napoleon

I wondered who had cherished it
This portrait he'd made
How long he'd been forgotten – till
Beneath the hammer laid

I don't suppose I'll ever know
About him, or his name
I only bought the photograph
So I could get the frame!

Justice

The mid-Victorian court was sat
The atmosphere was chill
The woman standing in the dock
Looked thin, and worn, and ill

A gentleman in spotless wig
With authority, he said
'Your crime is very serious
You stole a loaf of bread'

She cried, 'My mam is dead
I'd no money, not a farthing
I was desperate . . . I could see
My little children starving'

The judge then gave his sentence
Law and order must prevail
'This wretched thieving's got to stop
I'm sending you to jail'

The woman sobbed, 'My children
No food, no home, no bed'
Her pleas passed by unheeded
Here . . . charity was dead

The judge then checked his timepiece
'Let the other cases wait
I'm guest at the Lord Mayor's banquet
And it's bad manners to be late'

November 5th

Guido Fawkes, a gentleman
And a Yorkshire one at that
Before you burn your effigy
Please kindly raise your hat

He only went to Parliament
To spring a grand surprise
To keep the MPs nice and warm
And give them all a rise

Tempus Fugit

I hear the old clock
With his friendly tick tock
As his pendulum swings
To and fro
With his musical chime
As he fingers the time
To show where the hours
All go

He rings out the time
This old pal of mine
Though one thing is odd
I must say
For a diligent worker
Who's never a shirker
I hear that he strikes
Every day

It behoves me to mention
He needs little attention
Just a polish, or dust
Now and then
And if ever he clogs
Put some oil on his cogs
And he'll be ticking his old
Self again

Though affection he'll bring
His heart's only a spring
His face is impassive

And flat
His tummy reveals
Just a number of wheels
Which turn about this way
And that

So whirring away
His little wheels say
'Here's an end to your
Little rhyme.
Please be so kind
As to give me a wind
And we'll all have a jolly
Good time'

The Brook

Resting upon the heather
. . . we see the brook
In twilight's glow
Rushing, tumbling, prancing, dancing
Splashing, sparkling, springing
Swirling, singing
Leaping
Into the valley below

New Testament – Acts 5:1–11

You've heard of Ananias
An Israelite of old
At telling people untruths
He left the others cold.
If I were to write and his epitaph
I'd make it short and lucid

'Here lies Ananias'
Because, according to my Bible
This is all he ever did

The Violin

Standing in the corner
As if punished for a sin
A sorry sight indeed to see
An old and broken violin

His once firm joints are parting
The gloss and shine all gone
His strings have all been broken
All of them . . . save one

His former days of glory
Are now but just a dream
How sweet had been the melodies
Beneath the arc-lights' gleam

How silent all the listeners
To the music that he brings
Each note floats out so gently
As if on angels' wings

How often brought his sweet tone
A tear in many an eye
How many music lovers
With ecstasy would sigh

How sad the concert's over
How ill-fortune seems to gloat
Hear a 'ping', the last string's gone
A last discordant note

When in Doubt

At the bottom of the garden
In repose . . . a compost heap
A battered, tired, wooden hut
The garden tools to keep

Lumps of wood, a few old bricks
Lengths of wire, some rusty tin
Things we keep with good intent
Things we keep that might come in

Unlikely place one would think
To find a fairy bower . . . yet
Ancient legends and belief
Say this is where they flower

How often I, at mother's knee
In wide-eyed wonder stood
As she recited fairy tales
And stirred my childish blood

Now childish years are far behind
But magic ever clings . . .
Mystic thoughts of long ago
Through memory softly wings

On this warm and friendly evening
There's a strangeness in the air
Some haunting, pleasant sadness
Has caught me unaware

Perhaps I'll take a gentle stroll
To the garden down below
Though I don't believe in fairies
Then again . . . you never know!

11th November

Understand me when I say
That I have lost the will to pray
In church or at the cenotaph
On this . . . remembrance day

In Flanders' fields of red and green
Grey the crop of headstones seen
I stood amid the graveyard neat
And pondered how it might have been

I hear a weeping mother say
'With faith each night I knelt to pray'
Yet . . . like rainfall in the gutter
Her hopes were washed away

How much mercy to allow?
To English wife or German Frau
If they wouldn't listen then
Why should they listen now?

Despite the prayers from either side
However much for help we cried
A deathly silence from above
As hope and faith and young men died

Though we may be on bended knee
A stony silence greets our plea
Though we seek a guiding light
We look in vain a light to see

We pray that those who dwell above
Will care for them with heavenly love
But where the blessings so divine
Where, oh where, the peaceful dove?

Understand me when I say
Why should we . . . to heaven pray
. . . blindly follow, when it seems
The heavens too have lost their way

Winter

Winter has fled
His pallid face of snow
Has crying run
Before the armour bright
Of higher, rising sun
No more its chilling arms
Enfold our quivering flesh
The fields which covered 'neath
Its arid frozen breath
Are gaily blooming . . . fresh
Where grass and flowers
Raise their waiting heads
To warming, summer showers
Yet . . . skulking near he waits
With icy spear to hand
Until . . . by tilting globe
Sun's rays are cast awry
Then will he strike
His hordes once more . . .
This cruel, frozen band
East wind at their back
They will attack
Though autumn will resist
Just for a while
It will succumb
And once again
This bitter season will
A kind of beauty mime
As all is greyly trimmed
In winter's freezing rime

A Case of Mistaken Identity

A gentleman with a hairy chest
And hairs upon each leg
He'd none upon his head, of course
It looked just like an egg

A broody hen – not very bright
Thought she'd like to hatch it
And hoping for a little chick
Commenced a long and patient sit

The hen passed many years away
Sitting there like that
The gentleman was quite content
She made a lovely hat!

Gluttony

Fill the wine glass just enough
From pleasure don't refrain
Filled until it overflows
The tablecloth will stain

Dilemma

Pity the restless wanderer
Who falls in love one day
His legs will long to travel
But his heart will wish to stay

Sarajevo – 28th June 1914

The bullet fired, the weapon jerked
One more life was gone
The victim stopped the bullet
But the recoil carried on

A Dicky Bird

A dicky bird upon a tree
Sweetly sang . . . a song to me

He sang of lovely summer days
Of lambs at play, and cows that graze

How I loved his sweet refrain
I hope he'll sing to me again

One Day Whilst Out Walking

One day whilst walking in the park
A romping dog began to bark
A little girl was passing by
And, frightened, soon began to cry
On hearing this, the dog was sad
Began to wag his tail like mad
This was its way of making clear
That she had not a thing to fear
Though little girls are very sweet
They're not the things that doggies eat

What's-his-name

Pity the poet who never is found
By fame and fortune never crowned
Each and every chosen word
Never spoken, never heard

Maidens . . . villains, and the rose
All poured out in rhyme or prose
To lie and fade in dusty drawer
Till finally gone . . . lost . . . no more

To never know enduring fame
As that poet 'by another name'
We know by such a simple quote
From-out the countless words he wrote

Yet, if it filled an hour of leisure
Bringing then, some inward pleasure
Using time that may have bored
It surely brought its own reward

None so Fair

Sweet fragrance of love
This thornless rose
I twine within your hair
Blushing pink and shy
Among the strands so fair

Yet, in a heart and eye I know
Ne'er blooms a flower
Though free from moral flaws
That can . . . enhance
A beauty such as yours

Lesser Celandine

Lesser celandine (*ranunculus ficaria*) early spring
O' lovely flower . . . with which design
Nature will our hearts entwine
Though words may flow like vintage wine
No poet is born who can define
This hedgebanks' gem . . . so pure, so fine
The modest golden celandine

The Outing

A sailor boy went off to sea
In his sailor coat
He took a cat, he took a dog
He also took a goat
Unhappily they all got wet;
He forgot to take the boat!

Beauty's Glance

The snake is so revolting
To the likes of you and me
But to a lover of his species
How charming he must be

The Unknown Soldier – Circa AD 32

Strong and martial he stands
This soldier of Rome
A conqueror in an alien land
Far from his native home

The solemn night was lighted
By moonlight sallow glow
To this sentry cold and chill
The night was passing slow

He looked and saw
With indifferent eye
The cross outlined against the sky
And heard the muffled quaver
Of those who knelt and prayed beneath
To the one they called the saviour

Upon this everlasting scene
He glanced with bored disdain
But none but God
Shall ever . . . know his name

For Valour

How nice to be a hero
All my medals in a row
To shed my blood with valour
Against the foreign foe

I'd be a general if I could
I'm sure that must be good
For then I'd get the medals
By shedding someone else's blood

A Brave Young Man

A brave young man from Lorraine
To Paris he went on the train
Though the weather was grim
He went for a swim
The poor lad must be in Seine

Punny Question

Do sarcastic ghosts
Have the best taunts?

Faith, Hope and Charity

Faith is a smile on a saint's tortured face
Faith is a guide, to the human race
Faith is a dogma, that never diverts
Faith is an anchor, when the pain really hurts
Faith is a warrior, who knows no defeat
Faith is a fortress, in which many retreat
Faith is a prayer, that seeks no reply
Faith is a bulwark, we never ask why

Hope is the drug, that dulls our pains
Hope in disaster, is all that remains
Hope is the light, when the sun lowers its head
Hope gives us comfort, though the morning is red
Hope is the dream, in which we believe
Hope is the siren, who'll often deceive
Hope is the spirit, that urges us on
Hope is the staff, we all lean upon

Charity's a gesture, by those who donate
Charity's the sop, that breeds envy and hate
Charity's the fodder, to the cow who's been
    milked
Charity's the conscience, of the satined and silked
Charity's the pill, that prolongs the disease
Charity's the poison, which brings pride to its
    knees
Charity's the sneer, on a capitalist's face
Charity's the temptress, though false, we embrace

Sensibility

What use a butterfly's colours
A rainbow shining bright
Without the precious . . .
. . . gift of sight

What use the perfume of a flower
Its aroma to deploy
Without the means we all possess
Its fragrance to enjoy

What use to lovers hand-in-hand
Sweet lips so tender kissed
Without a sense of feeling
Such pleasures sorely missed

What use a soothing lullaby
Its soft, sweet melody
If no one hears its sweet refrain
How futile it would be

What use this Earth . . . and
All creatures here upon
Unless there's someone . . . somewhere
Looking on

Secrets

Remember us when we were young
And you were not yet twenty
How our hearts were always full
For we had love in plenty

Remember us when we were young
The things that we would say
At eventide within the copse
As on the grass we lay

Remember us when we were young
And strolled down Lovers' Lane
How I held and kissed you once
And kissed you once again

Remember us when we were young
In sunshine and in showers
How, parted by a lovers' tiff
We'd waste those precious hours

Remember us when we were young
My timorous . . . 'Would you?'
How you shyly bowed your head
And all my dreams came true

Yes . . . I remember. I remember
I remember very well
I remember all those things
But I will never tell

31st October (Candles and Turnips)

The sun has gone, the moon is high
The sort of night when witches fly

A chill wind's moaning, through the trees
A night to make the blood to freeze

Terror's riding on this wind
Seeking out the ones who've sinned

The superstitions lie a-bed
Beneath the sheets they hide their head

A festival of saints they say
But tonight would force the saints to pray

See those yellow turnip faces
Ghastly, glowing, cold grimaces

A more fearsome night is never seen
Than this the night of hallowe'en

Grandchildren

How nice they are when they are small
Will they be nice when they are tall?
Behind those gaily smiling eyes
No base deceits, no gainful lies
Watch them play with toys we bought
The giving which such pleasure brought
Happy, shining, healthy faces
When we meet our vision graces
Guileless is the message sent
A greeting and a compliment
Lips so sweet and innocent
Happily are curving sent
Upturned crescents
Free from wiles, welcome happy kiddies' smiles
Alas how purity from childhood
From childhood to maturity
To struggle with the human race
Their hopes and fears to embrace
And if in changing something's gone
Some things we built our image on
This transformation I'll regard
As natural . . . though seeming hard
As spins the coin, as rolls the ball
They are but human after all
Whatever fates may dispense
Warmth or cold indifference
I shall turn my inner gaze, with memories . . .
Of former days
And lovingly, I will recall . . .

How nice they were when they were small

I Made One

I remember when, my footsteps strayed
Within the copse where quietly played
Woodland creatures, who, enhanced the scene
Where shadowed paths were edged in green
Whilst as I slowly strolled along
Birds in chorus, voiced their song
I felt the cool, refreshing breeze
As in my mind a question formed
Could accident . . . create all these?

Within a quiet woodland glade
I saw a myriad patterns sprayed
Through the leaves the sunlight gleams
All my world is filled with dreams
A flickering magic lantern show
Lit only by celestial glow
Where wild, untended flowers grow
Or, perhaps, a gardener toils unseen
The question then is . . . who?

Perhaps the answer's all around
In nature where the signs abound
The sunshine and refreshing showers
The bee that pollinates the flowers
Compost from the golden shawl
Of autumn leaves, spread over all
The wind, the sower of the seeds
Guided by mysterious powers
Each season works . . . and then recedes

When winter with its icy wreath
Of snow . . . preserving all beneath
Has passed, and everywhere is is green and gold
And lovers' hearts are true and bold
I shall return with joy and verse
To ponder on this universe
And of creation thereupon
Though answer I may never find
Happy am I, that I made one

Insomnia

Why . . . do I not sleep?
These restless limbs, twisting and turning
I am warm, I have eaten
No wife, no children have I beaten
What guilty secret in my mind is burning
What is this vigil that I keep

Why . . . do I not sleep?
Restless thoughts that spring from restless days
What evil did I do, or say?
Just another humdrum day
Why does my mind ever wander through this
    maze?
Perhaps the answer lies too deep

Why . . . do I not sleep?
Do I live selflessly while others strive
Give the wrong gods preference
Offend them with indifference
These wandering thoughts, which keep my mind
    alive
These thoughts I sow, but cannot reap.

Time and Tide

Old ways, old bases
New ways, new phases
    How mixed
    Life's maze is

Old clothes, old laces
New clothes, new crazes
    How fast
    life's pace is

Old people, old faces
New people, new gazes
    How short
    Life's race is

Hardwicke

There on the fell side . . . cropping grass
. . . I see a lonely sheep
She turns her head to stare
. . . as noisily we pass
Our boots scrape on the rubble track,
As we wander in her moorland home . . .
I also . . . turn my head . . .
And stare . . . blankly back,
Two different worlds amongst the green
. . . a trivial moment of time,
Soon to be forgotten . . . as we,
Approach another scene,
The ewe, she'll graze with seeming leisure
. . . thoughts of us will surely fade,
But I shall remember this moment . . . which,
Gave me . . . so much pleasure

Kismet

Awake! Our vigil keep

The day is dawning
We play all through the morning

Childhood passes soon
We work all through the afternoon

Age gives way to youth receding
We rest awhile for it is evening

With steady hand, turn down the light
We are tired now and it is night

And we must sleep

Nostalgia

Echoes of my childhood
Whispers, with a sigh
Hazy pictures flickering
Across the inward eye

On sleepless nights . . . remembered
Spanning all the years
Dampening my pillow . . . with
Sweet and bitter tears

England

Bright sun is warming
Honey bees swarming
Church bells ringing
Worshippers singing
Hedgerows well groomed
Wild flowers perfumed
Sunday in June
Birds all in tune
This is my pleasure
Walking at leisure
This is my home . . . And
England's my homeland

Diary

Alas! Sly time has sneaked away the years
Turned the diary of my life, swiftly page by page
Robbed me of my youth, till grey and bent with
    age
With only memories to recall
Of happiness and tears

Limerick

I knew an old man who had a bald head
Not a hair to be seen . . . 'tis true to be said
No use for hair cream on that shiny dome
No use for a brush, no use for a comb
He uses furniture polish instead   [BY WINNIE]

Limerick

There was a young man named Gough
He had a terrible cough
He smoked fifty a day
And strange to say
They still haven't carried him off

Sarcasm

Were I a wit, with merry chaff
And phrases barbed and humorous
I think . . . though I could raise a laugh
My friends would not be numerous

29th May (Restoration) Oak Apple Day

The oak from a small acorn grows
As every English schoolchild knows
This was, of course, a lucky thing
For Charles Stuart, a would-be king

Ambitious for to wear the crown
He marched his men to Worcester town
But there his journey soon was stopped
By men whose hair was closely cropped

His ambition failed, we know because
He couldn't relish Worcester Sauce
(Please forgive the dreadful pun)
I'm only writing this for fun

Yet being caught was not his forté
He'd be chastised for being naughty
And to his father's fate took heed
Turned and fled at royal speed

He must quickly find a hiding place
So up an oak tree he did race
And there amongst its leaves so green
Hoped that he'd remain unseen

Cromwell's soldiers searched and searched
As Charlie up the tree was perched
And stayed 'til all was clear
This not so merry cavalier

Some years later, roundheads groan,
Charlie won the English throne,
The puritans their leader missed,
And the cavaliers – they all got hissed!

But a legacy he left behind
As on the inn-signs you will find
To commemorate the royal bloke
Some pubs were called The Royal Oak

So, if a royalist you would be
Keep Charlie in your memory
And don't forget this monarch gay
And celebrate oak apple day

Pendle Country

In a village midst the northern hills
Where witches once held sway
There is a weird tale can be told
But not explained away

This story new I will relate
A story strange but true
That started through the rumours
Which just grew and grew and grew

The lady at the post office
(Which served as village store)
Was quite convinced about it all
But said, 'I'll say nu moar'

That something pretty awful
Was going on . . . no doubt
The only mystery seemed to be
What was it all about?

Now the vicar he felt duty bound
To stop this sort of thing
And decided that to stamp it out
His influence he'd bring

First the vicar let it known
Around . . . to all and sundry
That he would give a special talk
In church, this coming Sunday

Now rumours can be harmful
And can be full of lies
So it seems that his decision
Was nothing . . . if not wise

The little church was amply full
For this extra special sermon
As one old lad was heard to say
'It'd better be a firm-un'

Now all the regulars were agreed
His rhetoric verged on rotten
But the vicar's sermon on that day
Will never be forgotten

He spoke with all the fire and verve
Of a man who was possessed
Of all the sermons ever preached
This surely was his best

He implored the wrath from up above
And from that place beneath
Some said his fiery oratory . . . was
Enough to scorch his teeth

Fire and brimstone, would reward
The sinners, they must know
Unless they changed their nasty ways
They'd end up down below!

He raised his arms in mock appeal
He raved and beat his breast
And all the listeners were agreed.
'By gum, he's done his best'

At last the service was at end
The last hymn had been sung
And if a bell there was to ring
It surely had been rung

The congregation filed from church
There'd ne'er been such demand
To praise him for his service
And shake the prelate's hand

But one old lady, wise with time
Was heard to say, 'Dear me,
Such a sermon's tempting fate
Mark my words; you'll see'

Some they laughed, others scoffed
'She all'us 'es bin queer.'
. . . folk, they took more heed
Well! They once had witches here

Though many vicars tend to pray
Both mentally and actual
None before had been known
To disturb the supernatural

This quite unusual . . . risky deed
It seems he had achieved, and
What happened next had to be seen
If it was to be believed

The wind began to howl and scream
Lightning flashed and roared
All around turned black as ink
And down the raindrops poured

The congregation strolling home
Ran off helter-skelter
Some teetotallers even dashed
Into the pub for shelter

'Me cellar's full o' watter'
Some heard the landlord say
A local wit cried, 'Never mind
It's allus bin that way'

Some reg'lars in the public bar
Considered it a treat
Said hopefully, 'If this keeps up
We'll 'ave ter stay all neet'

They say that Mrs Turnbull's cat
(It was the Persian kind)
Ran so fast to get indoors
It left its tail behind

Other yarns about that day
Are often still related
Some are true; others . . . well
Perhaps exaggerated

If by chance you pass that way
And the tales you'd like to hear
Codgers at the village pub, they say
React to pints of beer!

All in all, it was agreed
When at last the storm had ended
That calling on the powers that be
Could not be recommended

Of course the man, about the storm
To ask, it was quite plain . . .
The vicar, he's . . . the only one
This matter to explain

But sad it is, a sorry thing
The knowledge to evince
The vicar vanished in the storm
And no one's seen him since

Where he's gone no one knows
Who took their reverend brother
Upon one thing they all agreed
''Twas surely one or t'other'

Look After the Pennies

Look after the pennies, and pounds will
Look after themselves. Or . . .
Penny wise; pound foolish

Proverb

Penny Wise, a pleasant girl
Very fond of saving
She wasn't mean, but drew the line
At borrowing and lending

Such a method would, it seems
Lead to great contentment
Alas . . . she only saved the pence
All her pounds were quickly spent

From this, I think, we must agree
Her results were pretty poorish
Although she . . . was Penny Wise
She also was pound foolish

Like most proverbs, these two are
A work of complete fiction
As one can very clearly see
They lead to contradiction

So if you really would be wise
And build a nest-egg with your pence
Forget all the proverbs you have heard
Just use some commonsense

Ambiguity

The form in which . . . the willow bends
An air of sadness lends . . .
Yet . . . from out so many throats
. . . Of birds
. . . Their joyous notes
This gloom transcends
And with the sparkling river . . .
. . . Dancing by
The sun is high
The summer's countryside
The insects hum . . . the fishes glide
If then . . . there is a sigh
Amongst this trove of treasure . . .
. . . It must surely be
A sigh of pleasure

The Playing Cards

The hour's late, the players tired
To continue they weren't able
They left the cards all spread around
As we begin our fable
They left the cards all spread around
Upon the green baize table

But as the midnight hour chimed
The fateful moves began
As, silently, each set of cards
All faithful to a man
As, silently, each set of cards
To their royal masters ran

Each King set up his royal court
Each King thought he should rule
Alas with stupid arrogance
More suited to a mule
Alas with stupid arrogance
Each thought the other King a fool

The King of Spades said, full of spite
'We Spades, we are the workers
I'm the one, the one to rule
We'll tolerate no shirkers.
I'm the one, the one to rule
Take care who would oppose us'

The King of Diamonds – very rich
Was quick to disagree:
'I should rule; without my wealth
You'd all be poor, you see.
I should rule; without my wealth
Wherever would you be?'

The King of Clubs cried out in a rage
'Your plans aren't very bright
We are the ones well armed you know
We have the clubs with which to fight
We are the ones well armed you know
And soon you'll see that might is right'

Said the King of Hearts, a kindly man
May all his kind increase
'I think that commonsense should reign
Let all this quarrelling cease
I think that commonsense should reign
Then we could live in peace

His words of wisdom were ignored
As they justified his fears
The King of Hearts was sad and wept
And soon a flood appears
The King of Hearts was sad and wept
And drowned in his tears!

The waters fast subsided
And soon the search was on
Alas the King could not be found
They'd crossed the Rubicon!
Alas the King could not be found
The King of Hearts had gone

The gamblers came back rested
Once more they'd like to play
When they found a card was missing
They all voiced their dismay
When they found a card was missing
They threw the pack away

All fifty-one they threw away
The cards all on the fire
Soon burned to ashes, they became
It was their funeral pyre

The moral of this tale is clear
Don't rant and rave and rail
Discuss your problems sensibly
Don't let reason fail
Discuss your problems sensibly
Let sanity prevail

Who Am I?

I sat in solitude
And I spoke
Hoping
Some answers to evoke . . .
. . . From out the air
. . . For this is where
Christians
In their zeal
Assure me that
I must appeal

The question was . . .
'Who am I?'
From the distance
Came no reply
Heard only was
The echo of my voice:
'Who am I?'
I waited . . . and
Once more did try
Once more
Echo answered
'Who am I?'

Sadly I learn
How ever long I sit
The void asks only
What I ask of it

Pollution

Willow tree, why are you weeping
On this lovely summer's day?
O'er the grassy banks your tendrils reaching
Grasping for the tumbling waters
As the river wends its way

Willow tree, sad vigil keeping
Whilst songbirds sing so gay
This harvest gold you should be reaping
As the bright warmth of the sun
Helps the dark clouds fade away

Willow tree as downward glancing
See the waters – grim and grey
The deathless dance beneath you prancing
As the lifeless billows flow
I shall weep with you today

The Yorkshire Dales (and Hills)

These Yorkshire Dales
This shawl of green
Spread o'er England's shoulders
Patterned bright with polka dots
Of sheep, and limestone boulders

On rugged hills
Through gentle vale
Drystone walls meander
A chequerboard of grey and green
Which makes the heart grow fonder

Quiet villages
In history set
To their verdant bosom pressed
The rivers flow so sweetly . . . where
The fell sides came to rest

In this landscape set
In nature's crown
I would for ever wander
Excited by their rural charm
Subdued by all their grandeur

Primroses

There's a place I know where as a boy
Playtime hours I spent with joy
Two grassy banks of verdant green
A little stream that ran between

An old mill with its crumbling piers
Derelict for many years
Once a working place for men
Became a small boy's private den

In spring the grassy banks would show
Primroses bright . . . in yellow glow
Happy the memory of the hours
I spent amongst the lovely flowers

I know, of course, I'll not return
To those grassy banks and pretty burn
Nostalgia burns within me bright
But reality may dim the light

What use are memories we may say
What use the thoughts of a bygone day
My legacy from a bygone hour
The primrose yet . . . my favourite flower

On the Sculpture, 'Prospector'
created by William Elphick

His battered hat
With upturned brim
His bearded visage
Worn and grim
A wanderer
Now grown old
In his relentless search for gold

At belted waist
A gun and knife
Reflecting on
A dangerous life
Rock-strewn landscape
Round his feet
The larger rock a welcome seat

We must imagine
What he sees
Work-worn hands
Rest on his knees
His dusty clothes
Look drier than
The arid stream
He hoped to pan

The little 'burro'
Standing near
Attentive seems
Each outspread ear
Neck thrust where
It may think
The dish may hold
A cooling drink

His worldly goods
Upon his back
Shovel and picks
And bedding sack
Water bottle
And billycan
The spartan gear
Of a spartan man

The sculptor has created here
A monument
Of yesteryear
With bronze and skill
Can his creation
But evoke
Appreciation?

Sounds

The sounds of summer
The sound of a mowing machine
As it happily hums a gentle tune
Whilst mowing the grass so green

The swell of applause at a cricket match
The smack of a cricket ball hitting a bat
And when the game seems quiet and slow
A sudden loud chorus, to the umpire, 'How's
that?'

The drone of a jet plane . . . silvery bird
Traversing the heavens so high
To faraway places . . . whilst leaving behind
Fleecy white ribbons . . . across the blue sky

Steadily flying from flower to flower
The brown and gold striped busy bee
His familiar buzz, as he wends on his way
Is a sound that says . . . honey for tea

As it races off down the valley
The mountain stream, bubbling and gay
Fills my ears with its wonderful music
As it sings along its way

The lonely call of the curlew
Much rural pleasures can bring
Or the merry skylark
As he sings . . . and he soars . . . on the wing

The happy sound of the children
As they play through life long day
Enjoying the blessings of childhood
As life's journey starts on its way

The sound of a kettle boiling
To herald a warm cup of tea
Or the hiss of a landlord's beer tap
As he draws a cool pint . . . just for me

The nostalgic sound of the whistle
As the night train . . . flickering bright
Rushes on . . . until finally swallowed
By the dark, hungry mouth of the night

Willow Pattern

There besides the sparkling wine
A picture that I would define
This lovely blue and white design
A sailing boat glides o'er the sea
The centrepiece a willow tree
An illustration quite divine
Is that a lotus that I see?

Arched like a tiger set to spring
Bamboo bridge . . . in homage bending
Three people, on their way are wending
Walking o'er in single file
Gaily dressed in Chinese style
With the background nicely blending
Pagodas, temples . . . mystic isle

A zig-zag fence with lamps upon
White the path that leads me on
To a beautiful pavilion
Surrounded all by leaves and flowers
A picture wrought of scented bowers
This scene that breaths of 'halcyon'
Imparts a sense of magic hours

Two loving doves are flying high
This tale of love that would not die
Will cast a tear a breath a sigh
A tale of love with magic sent

To us . . . from out the Orient
And in the little rhyme shall I
This story tell of love's lament

A boy and girl, in summer, gay
As each was going on their way
They met upon the bridge one day
He smiles, and she her eyes did lower
And though they'd never met before
Predestined they their parts to play
They fell in love for evermore

But fate a cruel web did weave
That only mortals could conceive
This boy and girl they would deceive
For she was rich and he was poor
It was decreed they'd meet no more
And parted they must sadly grieve
As none have ever grieved before

But love will ever find a way
Though fate with human hearts may play
No bitter force their passion stay
Parted by the waters deep
They found a way their trysts to keep
It seems that nothing could gainsay
Their just reward to reap

Each would construct a paper boat
To safely on the billows float
Across the wide, forbidding moat
In each a loving message borne

To cheer these lovers all forlorn
A teardrop stains whereon they wrote
As their parting they would mourn

And as the gentle breeze would blow
Helped by the tidal ebb and flow
The paper boats sailed to and fro
Messages to him to her
Sweet nothings these their hearts will stir
For their true love they must show
Whatever wrath it may incur

At last in secret they did meet
Precious moments, short and sweet
But soon discovered, must retreat
To swim to safety they were bound
But sadly these two lovers drowned
To lie, it seemed, at Neptune's feet
Beneath the restless sound

And near the spot for all tomorrow
Drooping where the wavelets billow
The weeping willow bends in sorrow
Shedding tears for love that's gone
Tears enough for everyone
Who such a sorry path must follow
Or such a fate should fall upon

But wraiths of power in high degree
Omnipotent . . . they did decree
That such an end was not to be
Rewarding such devoted love

Each was charmed into a dove
To fly for all eternity
All earthly things . . . above

And now my story I have told
In memory of love to hold
A memory of love so bold
For ever they shall now remain
Immortalized in porcelain
Though fashioned all in clay and cold
Without the fire, no pot, no pain

Local Folk Song

What cared I for womenfolk
To while away the hours
I had a faithful cat and dog
My garden with its flowers

A pub just round the corner
Where the ale *still* freely flows
With local lads to chaff and chat
With darts and dominoes

A bachelor's life – a gay life
That was the life for me
No romance and no regrets
Footloose and fancy free

One day I met a lady fair
My resolve began to faulter
And human weakness must be blamed
That led me to the altar

Her female charms my passions roused
And I was soon a-wooing – but
'Before we bed, we wed,' she said
And that was my undoing

So now a married man am I
Just as happy as can be
I live in the pub, and everything's good
For the bride was the landlady

Where the Wind Blows

I am the wild wind
So happy and free
If your spirit could wander
Then wander with me

We'll whip around the houses
And rattle each pane
Then, over the rooftops
And off, down the lane

Let's have some fun
With the girls passing by
Make them hold down their hats
As their dresses fly high

Away through the woodlands
We'll breathe soft and low
Where the sweet celandine
And the primroses grow

Then over the seas
Where the tall ships glide
We'll fill up their sails
'Til they're bulging with pride

The wandering albatross
On our currents will ride
O'er limitless oceans
With wings spreading wide

The waters so calm
Before we passed by
Are changed in a moment
The waves heaving high

We'll blast to the north
Where the reindeer roams
And eskimos crouch
In quaint igloo homes

Perhaps to the tropics
Where palm trees grow
Watch coconuts fall
As we bustle and blow

Then off to the west
Where red indians ride
On their ponies . . . across
The prairie so wide

We'll waft round his wigwam
And tall totem pole
And pick up the dust
Where the wagon trails roll

With hardly a breath
Once more we're away
To the pagodas and temples
Of distant Cathay

See the great wall of China
Built so long ago
And blow Chinese junks
Up the might Hwang-ho

We'll storm round the globe
'Til we've had our fill
The world is our oyster
To swallow at will

Then back over Europe
Our zephyrs will roam
Though grand is our journey
It's nice to come home

. . . To reaching church spires
Midst a patchwork of green
The weathervanes point
To the places we've been

To England, our England
There we would be
Where rolling, green meadows
Mean homeland to me

With the south wind a-blowing
There we'll come to rest
Like birds of adventure
Flown home to their nest

Senses of . . .

I speak to you and
   I know
My words paint on your cheeks . . . a
   rosy glow

I hear your voice
   a violin
Which charms my heart . . . you
   must win

I smell your fragrance
   and delight
In perfume sweet as blossoms . . . of
   the night

I touch your hand
   and feel
A warmth that makes . . . my
   senses reel

I look into your eyes
   and see
A light of love that . . . shines
   for me

. . . love

The Bad Guy

There lived a rough, tough hombre
His name was Black M'Graw
He was a killer without mercy
He was wanted by the law

He wore a pair of six guns
Slung low down on his thighs
He paralysed his victims
With his cold and snake-like eyes

Each gun, upon the handle
Was scarred with notches deep
A record of his victims
For Black M'Graw to keep

One victim, he a pious man
By religion was a Quaker
Before he'd time to say 'Amen'
He'd gone to meet his maker

Another one an Indian brave
You won't see him around
Black M'Graw has dispatched him
To his happy hunting ground

And there were lots of sheriffs
Alas! They've all gone dead
They traded shots with Black M'Graw
Who filled them full of lead

What a dreadful story
But now I must relate
How in a town, way out west
This villain met his fate

He tangled with an unknown man
And challenged him to fight
Who killed M'Graw, then silently
Rode off into the night

They buried him just out of town
Beneath a little mound
And written on his headstone
This legend can be found:

Here it lies, God rest his soul
The body of Black M'Graw
One day he met a stranger
Who was faster on the draw

Newspaper Competitions

Like Aladdin with his lamp
I explored the magic cave
Gold nor jewels did I find
Just silence . . . cold and damp

A Little Girl

A little girl, her name Louise
One day she gave a mighty sneeze
And then she gave a mighty cough
Blew brother Robert's hat right off
His hat flew high up in the air
It flew so high he knew not where
Now Robert he was quite surprised

He looked amazed, with open eyes
Louise then said, 'I'll tell you what
Look, it's up there on the chimney pot'
Of course, they couldn't climb so high;
And, no, of course, they couldn't fly
So there it stays where it came to rest
The birds now use it as a nest

Original

The golden sun . . . sinks in the west
And I feel sure that way's the best
If it sank in the east – wonders never cease –
Indians and the cowboys, why?
They'd all be Chinese

A Wishing Well

A wishing well, the story goes
It was told me by a fish
Throw your penny down the pit
And then you make a wish

A miser who was very rich
One day . . . passing by
Hoping for some plump reward
Thought he'd have a try

Took a penny from his purse
But I regret to tell
Was too greedy to let it go
And fell into the well

Having paid his penny
He began to shout
Hoped his wish be granted
That someone got him out

A Walking Stick

A walking stick was in its stand
He was waiting for his master
They went into the park each day
And listened to the band

In common with all other sticks
He was thin and at an angle
He also had quite a long nose
Which made a lovely handle

Upon the end that touched the ground
He had a rubber tip
Which came in very useful . . . when
There were spots where he might slip

He always felt important
As they went on their way
Waving at his master's friends
And shooing dogs away

And so they went a-roaming
Down vale and over hill
And I think that if you see them
You'll find them walking still

I Wonder Why

I wonder why a cat likes milk
Why babies' cheeks are soft as silk
Why a mouse is fond of cheese
Why pepper always makes us sneeze

I wonder why the stars shine bright
And why the sun goes in at night
Why eskimos live in the snows
And never where the palm tree grows

I wonder why the grass grows green
And out of sight . . . cannot be seen
Why music enters in our ears
And sorrow comes out with our tears

Why Africans are black as night
Whilst others are yellow, brown and white
Why Santa's cloak . . . has a white edge
And why he always rides a sledge

I wonder why the birds fly high
And don't fall down like you and I
Why great oaks from acorns grow
Is something else I'd like to know

Why the lightning, why the thunder
Why all these questions you may wonder
It's simply that I'd like to find
The answers . . . and some peace of mind

The Tip
Or, the Wandering Thoughts of a Wondering Waiter

First
The customers, a ragged pair
Each sat upon a vacant chair
Ordered both in voice genteel
A cheap, but somewhat wholesome, meal

Now
The meal consumed, prepared to leave
How big a tip would I receive?
Gentlefolk they may be
But not too rich, 'twas plain to see

However
Just a common waiter I
Possessed with most discerning eye
How much a tip from such a pair
Could one expect, being fair

But
Should I refuse
A tip, of course,
This could make the matter worse
Their offering briskly turned aside
Would hurt, I'm sure, their misplaced pride

Agreed
The service I had carried out
'Twas my duty, there's no doubt
For which the master, he will pay
Come the reckoning Saturday

Though
Whose need would seem greater
A point that I'd consider later
Whatever conscience may deplore
I'd be richer than before

Alas
Oh that I could strength incur
Decline the coins that they proffer
But poverty and simple greed
Pays my conscience little heed

Finally
With difference
Due to such largesse
With practised hand, and great finesse
Obsequious-palm produced with ease
I bow, my honoured guests to please

Once Upon a Summertime

O' lovely, lovely summer's day
To pause and wile the time away
Let nature take me by the hand
Guide me through her wonderland

All my cares drift slowly by
As in the verdant grass I lie
Recumbent, happy, silent, still
To the skylarks' song I thrill

I feel warming zephyrs pass
See the shimmering quivering grass
Hear a gentle rustle then
All is quiet once again

In my vision treetops show
Swaying, dancing to and fro
Shaking every friendly leaf
As though to nod at me beneath

High above calm and cool
Blue, the sky, a swimming pool
In which the swallow dips and dives
Dolphin of the summer skies

A dragonfly suspended there
As if by magic in the air, to pose
A butterfly of many hues
Did this fleeting moment choose

A cowslip near my grassy bed
Humbly bows her golden head
As though shy the sun to face
Whilst nestling in its warm embrace

I close my eyes in reverie
Eavesdrop on a buzzing bee, though
Sweet the nectar from the flower
Less sweeter than this golden hour

Poem from Albert (1937)

Oh to wander down a country lane
In the twilight's softening hour
Come daylight the world is plain
But evening with its magic power
Whispers softly to the soul

To see the sun sink down
A flaming gold, majestic mass
Or then to hear as shadows frown
The trees and little blades of grass
Murmuring of the day just past

To pause, and ponder themes of things
Why these rapturous moments not be tied
With firmer bonds than memory's strings
Then in cheerless winter . . . loose them wide
In a flood of ecstacy

Dotty Definitions

Maiden voyage:
To boldly go,
Where no man's
Been before

Missile

Bullet, inconsiderate thing
Dangerous upon the wing
Alas, the one . . . it lights upon
Likely hurt, more likely . . . gone

Anagram

Wonderful the anagram
Can change an arm into a ram.
Lancaster, as we know well
Remains, of course, ancestral

Quotes

For quotable quotes I've a preference
    I read them
With suitable awe, and with reverence
    It seems
The words of the wise are very concise
Which perhaps accounts for their cleverness

No More Today

No more today
I will away
Over there
To my armchair

The Aristocracy Flickering in Our Democracy

On television screens he'll score
The privileged know all raconteur
And for a fee he won't disclose
He'll spout his educated prose
Tell us of his childhood days
With honest, upright, British gaze
Of Eton, or Harrow, or some public school
Where diction was taught the workers to fool
How at Cambridge he rowed upon the Cam
Whilst we survived on bread and jam
Should we of lesser lights complain
Because in his sheltered life he learned
Whilst we . . . stood in the rain

Should we like vandals ridicule
This . . . blue-blooded . . . prattling fool
Or like the audience laud and clap
This jolly 'good old' varsity chap
Perhaps negate his continued presence
As one should to all excrescence . . . No,
Like obedient puppies we sit up and beg
As he clucks and lays each verbal egg
Why then? He the what and we the who?
Perhaps the reason is painful but true
Why we are so poor and he is so rich
Plain is the answer if . . . we're too lazy
To rise . . . and turn off the switch

The Books

Five books on the library shelves
Began to talk amongst themselves
Each had a content and a colour
That differed somewhat from the other

The colours are all so plainly seen
Yellow and red and blue and green
To complete the five there on the rack
A book in sombre shade of black

The yellow book was first to speak
'To those who mystic guidance seek
I tell of gods and all their faces
And the fickle ways of human races'

The green book then gave a speech
'My pages into history reach
Great events from far and near
You will find them listed here'

The blue book next he'd have his say
'My tales are mixed: some sad, some gay
Some tell of evil . . . of love, even lust
Envy and jealousy . . . hate and mistrust'

The red book said, 'My pages will tell
Of mystery and murder, torture as well
Of battles in wartime, viciously fought
How victors and vanquished all came to nought'

The black book now the last to give voice
He solemnly said, 'Whatever the choice
Inside my volume how easy to find
All of your stories no matter which kind'

This gave the others occasion to look
All these situations in only one book
They read his gold title slightly in awe
The words *Holy Bible* were the words that they
    saw

Hill Billy – Cowboy Song
(pity about the music)

Will he was a cowboy
His life was just a song
With his old guitar and a tra-la-la
He'd gaily ride along
His songs were so infectious
The 'critters' all joined in
And when they got together
They made a rare old din
A lonely owl in that old barn
When Will sang, 'I love you,'
He joined in the chorus
With a 'Twit-a-wit-a-woo'

Now Will he was an orphan
He had no kith or kin
His Ma and Pa were his guitar
In life through thick and thin
Sometimes he rode the Chisholm trail
Herding cows and steers
He'd serenade them at night
To calm down all their fears.
Now them there cows they loved it all
When he sang of love so true
They'd all join in in the chorus
With a bovine, 'Moo-moo-moo'

Will never had a homestead
He was always one to roam
Beneath a star with his guitar

Was the place that he called home
He'd light his fire and cook his beans
Then sing of girls so 'purdy'
From far away in Monterey
Or even Albuquerque
Coyotes in the wilderness
They loved his singing too
And they'd all join in the chorus
With a barking, 'Woo-woo-woo'

Alas, poor Will has ridden on
His roaming days are done
With his guitar, he'd travelled far
Somewhere beyond the sun
And if at night you sit a spell
When the prairie's calm and still
Just lend an ear to heaven
And listen for old Will
His song trails down the moonbeams
To sing his fond adieu
Whilst angels, all in chorus, sing
Their halle-lu-oo-oo

Cat-a-logue

Cat-a-logue
Written purr-pussly because
Victoria told mee-ow much
she loved cats

There was a cat
It would appear
That had a grin
From ear to ear
Also a cat that had nine lives
And one like Alice
That went to the palace
And some on the way to St Ives

There's a cat you couldn't swing round a room
And one that sits
On a witch's broom
Dick Whittington he'd a famous cat
And, hey diddle
There was one on the fiddle
And one that sat on the mat

There are large cats like lions
And tigers too
Can safely be seen
If one goes to the zoo
Quarrelsome cats from kilkenny
As legends will tell
There's poor puss in a well
Oh dear, it seems there's so many

Cat-o'-nine tails
Not very nice
And cats that help
To keep down the mice
Pantomime has its Puss-in-Boots
There's also the cat that killed the rat
And some who are made into suits

There's also a cat
Who sat under a chair
I'm not sure when
I'm not sure where
Black cats are said to be lucky
Cats out of the bag
I'm beginning to flag
These cats are driving me potty

Cat on a hot tin roof
On hot bricks as well
Tail-less ones from the Isles of Man
Grey, brown and tortoiseshell
With dogs they came down as rain
To add to the score . . . There's
The ginger tom from next door
I think I'm going insane

There's Sylvester and Felix
Cartoons made famous
And in Ireland I'm sure
Is one named Seamus
There must be many I haven't mentioned

But here I will end
Or I'll go round the bend
There seems to be moggies galore

Pace Bowler

Summer sun so kind today
No rain or cloud to hold up play
As bowler walks to marker seen
Amid the distant spread of green

There he goes; see him wheel
Quickly turn, toe to heel
Start to run at steady pace
As if to start a longish race

Legs go faster; feet pound hard
Batsman takes determined guard
Keeper, umpire, fielders all
In homage crouch to bright, red ball

Bowler's reaching bowling crease
Soon his missile to release
There it goes, swings and jumps
Failure now and goodbye stumps

Batsman in his white-lined fort
Snicks the ball, 'Howzat?' He's caught
Straight into the fielder's hand
All in order, just as planned

Alas the fates, so unkind
Bowler sadly soon to find
Spinning ball falls to ground
From fielder's grip so unsound

Loud the silence seems to shriek
It seems to last . . . about a week
Fielder's face embarrassed, pink
How he longs in earth to shrink

One hand resting on his hip
Bowler stares at erring slip
Disbelief so plain to see
How could he do this to me?

To batsman too, a baleful glare
Expression says, 'Lucky there.'
Batsman does his party piece
Pats the ground before his crease

On with match, no time to grieve
Walking, rolls up fallen sleeve
On and on, to marker seen
Amid the distant spread of green

Index